SNAILS

by Meg Gaertner

Cody Koala

An Imprint of Pop!
popbooksonline.com

abdobooks.com
Published by Pop!, a division of ABDO, PO Box 398166, Minneapolis,
Minnesota 55439. Copyright © 2019 by POP, LLC. International copyrights
reserved in all countries. No part of this book may be reproduced in any
form without written permission from the publisher. Pop!™ is a trademark
and logo of POP, LLC.

Printed in the United States of America, North Mankato, Minnesota

092018
012019

THIS BOOK CONTAINS
RECYCLED MATERIALS

Cover Photo: iStockphoto
Interior Photos: iStockphoto: 1, 5 (top), 5 (bottom left), 6, 13, 15 (top), 15
(bottom left), 15 (bottom right); Robert J. Erwin/Science Source, 9, 10;
Shutterstock Images: 5 (bottom right), 16–17, 20; Francesco Tomasinelli/
Science Source, 19

Editor: Charly Haley
Series Designer: Laura Mitchell

Library of Congress Control Number: 2018950118
Publisher's Cataloging-in-Publication Data

Names: Gaertner, Meg, author.
Title: Snails / by Meg Gaertner.
Description: Minneapolis, Minnesota: Pop!, 2019 | Series: Pond animals |
    Includes online resources and index.
Identifiers: ISBN 9781532162107 (lib. bdg.) | ISBN 9781641855815 (pbk) |
    ISBN 9781532163166 (ebook)
Subjects: LCSH: Snails--Juvenile literature. | Pond snails--Juvenile literature.
    | Pond animals--Juvenile literature.
Classification: DDC 594.38--dc23

Hello! My name is
Cody Koala

Pop open this book and you'll find QR codes like this one, loaded with information, so you can learn even more!

Scan this code* and others like it while you read, or visit the website below to make this book pop.

popbooksonline.com/snails

*Scanning QR codes requires a web-enabled smart device with a QR code reader app and a camera.

Table of Contents

Freshwater Snails

Snails are small animals with soft bodies and hard shells. They live all over the world.

Watch a video here!

There are more than 65,000 kinds of snail. About 5,000 of these live in freshwater areas. These areas include ponds, lakes, and **marshes**.

Chapter 2

Life in a Shell

A snail carries a shell on its back. The outside of the shell is rough. But the inside is soft. This way the shell does not hurt the snail's soft body.

Learn more here!

A snail's head has one or two **pairs** of **tentacles**. The snail's mouth is between them. Many snails have eyes on their tentacles.

Snails have thousands of tiny teeth.

A snail has one foot. The foot is covered with tiny bumps called cilia. They help the snail move. The rest of the snail's body is inside its shell.

shell

eyes

tentacles

mouth

foot

Food and Safety

Most freshwater snails eat **algae**. They hide during the day. They come out at night to eat.

Learn more here!

Many **predators** eat
snails. This includes turtles,
fish, and birds.

To stay safe, a snail pulls its head and foot into its shell.

Chapter 4

Growing Up

Female snails lay eggs. They attach the eggs to rocks or logs. Some snails lay two eggs. Others lay more than 300 eggs.

Complete an activity here!

Snail eggs hatch fast in warm water. Baby snails are almost too small to see. But they grow a lot during their first year.

Snails can live two to 15 years.

Making Connections

Text-to-Self

Have you ever seen a snail in real life? If not, have you seen another animal in the wild?

Text-to-Text

Have you read another book about a different animal? How is that animal similar to a snail? How is it different?

Text-to-World

Snails use their shells to stay safe. How do other animals stay safe?

Glossary

algae – plants that live in ponds or lakes and that do not have stems, flowers, or roots.

female – a person or animal of the sex that can have babies or lay eggs.

marsh – wet land usually filled with grass or other plants, also called a swamp.

pair – a group of two.

predator – an animal that hunts and eats other animals.

tentacle – a flexible, moving limb.

Index

Online Resources

popbooksonline.com

Thanks for reading this Cody Koala book!

Scan this code* and others like it in this book, or visit the website below to make this book pop!

popbooksonline.com/snails

*Scanning QR codes requires a web-enabled smart device with a QR code reader app and a camera.